Announcements

Lauren Pope

Templar Poetry

Published in 2017 by Templar Poetry

Fenelon House
Kingsbridge Terrace
58 Dale Road, Matlock, Derbyshire
DE4 3NB

www.templarpoetry.com

ISBN 978-1-911132-31-8
Copyright © Lauren Pope 2017
Lauren Pope has asserted her moral right to be identified as the author
of this work in accordance
with the Copyright, Designs and Patents Act 1988

All rights reserved. This book is sold subject to the condition
that it shall not, by way of trade or otherwise, be lent, resold, hired out
or otherwise circulated without the publisher's prior consent, in any form
of binding or cover other than that in which it is published and without
a similar condition including this condition being imposed on
the subsequent purchaser

For permission to reprint or broadcast these poems write to
Templar Poetry

A CIP catalogue record of this book is available from the British Library

Typeset by Pliny

Cover Design and Artwork by Templar Design

Printed in England

Acknowledgements

Grateful acknowledgment is made to the following publications in which these poems, or versions of these poems, first appeared: *Etchings*, *Glasgow Review of Books*, *Gutter*, *Magma*, *Quotidian: A Literary Magazine*, *The Rialto*, *The Stockholm Review of Literature* and *The Undertow Review*. Special thanks to Miriam Gamble and Jane McKie for their support and guidance, and to the members of Poetry Gang for good company, comments and drink: Jonathan Bay, Tim Craven, Russell Jones, Marianne MacRae and Sarah Stewart.

for Ross

CONTENTS

Proverb — 1

Botanics — 2

My Sister's Epiphany — 4

Matins — 6

Locusts — 7

Confessional — 8

I can't feel my face when I'm with you… — 9

Pavement Vomit — 10

Man Whore — 11

Vile Jelly — 12

Petit Socco — 14

Exhibit A, Exhibit B — 16

After the Drought — 18

If You Love Him, Let Him Sleep — 19

Miscarriage — 20

More Asleep Than Dead — 22

Elegy of the Sandcastle — 23

Fractals of Depression — 24

Scar — 25

Backstage — 26

Metamorphosis — 27

My Father Tells Me to Get Married — 28

Mauna Loa — 30

Proverb

When you say, 'the fig that bleeds milk is not ripe,'
it sounds like a proverb. Through the window

I turn my head to better view our landscape. Gold grass hills
have beached around Vinci, and my mind goes to my hair —

bleached into brittle strands of straw, an obsession with light perhaps.
Still, like a niggle or a sting from a fire ant,

all I can think is that I don't like the way you're holding that fig,
the way it unsettles this moment, and others to come,

so that now, when your hand moves to my lower back,
I think of it as a root grounding me to you, an umbilicus.

My gaze settles on the walled geometry of a courtyard
and the male figure of a Roman statue, armless, inside.

Botanics

I held my breath,
wondering if
the Kadapul flower
would flirt
with evening —

stretch open
in one long
smoky
post-coital
yawn.

We listened
to the curator
describe flowers
as passing clouds;
mother passed
us water —

Stay hydrated,
we may be here a while —
as if we would wilt
without 8oz a day.

In the space
of her whisper
the blossom opened,
raised its head
towards death.

A feral tongue
blinked

within folds
of fanned pearl,
a spray of pollen
perfumed the air,

someone sneezed;
the deviant cackle
trailed from sight,

leaving
in its wake,
a pile
of crumpled
silk.

My Sister's Epiphany

She moves around the room,
in search of something,
like a hawk kiting on moderate wind
though not as graceful.

'Is the dying thing sad?'
        'Yes, generally the dying thing is sad.'

Mimic my cry. Watch how I shake hands,
listen for the crack in my smile—
it will be a faint noise, like the click of a lock

or the earth opening up.

Christina Maria is a shadow
at our granddaddy's funeral in Pocatello.
She repeats what our mother
shouted as she parked the car
and took out the casserole.

'mommy said we parked
       at the ass-end of space.'

The guests laugh, some sound like cotton balls,
others are nervous like the dirt waiting
to be discovered under the refrigerator.

She thinks she has made a joke, and repeats,
'ass-end of space.'

Then the room becomes quiet,
except for the kick of the drier's foetal contents

in the room adjoining the kitchen,
and a whisper—

'someday will I die?'
      'Yes, someday you will.'
'That will be sad.'

Matins

The day the *gringa*
gave birth to their daughter
he drank whiskey from a stranger's flask
on the back of a bus
from El Salvador to Texas
where he found the *mija* already swathed
in Lone Star orange, garish
next to the indigo of his country.

He drank the Texan way that night
with the *mamacita's* new man,
pronouncing Jameson with an 'h',
shortening it to 'hi-mé'
as the hours staggered by.

Jorge and Juan, saints
he had sculpted for the nursery
from the legs of old cathedral pews
were silent in his pocket;

he could just make out
the morning song of warblers
as they dipped
into the garden font.

Locusts

Remember
that swarm of intimacy –
our dinner table's crèche
held together by candlelight,
the ribbon of crepe stars
strung above us;

the way your lips mouthed 'nyama' -
tongue touching
your two front teeth –
the word for 'meat'
having more to do with me
than your meal;

how the first rain fell
during dessert
on a plate of pineapple
and a Milky Way melted
to its wrapper;

how, as the locusts
hatched, we listened
to their hind legs thrum –
like the white noise
of a TV left on?

Confessional

Stumbling in from hoarfrost   he enters
wet   and I know I could push him
    over   and leave him   lying
in a puddle
            of gin-infused sweat   skin corroding
the Fired Earth encaustic tiles
              in our doorway

      but I love those tiles
(we lived on tinned tomatoes   on toast
       and cooking wine
last winter   to pay for them)

Be less Dali's *Le Sommeil*   I want to say
His honesty stretches out   flat
        mine's   only just beginning

Among other transgressions   I keep my truths
so far down
          the spit mine

              mild trichophagia
                      his hand   that gropes me
          in his sleep

"I can't feel my face when I'm with you
        but I love it,
                but I love it."

The song of summer takes me —

and just like that, the memory
of the NOS tank we stole
from Pinky's Auto Mechanics
comes back to me: that bodily
form of weathering that cracked
us from freeze to thaw
with every hit
of the rubber lung;

the droplets from Brittany's nose
in a cochineal trail
across the bedroom carpet —
I may have cupped them
into something precious
or tried.

Pavement Vomit

A spilled gut spoils
in the light of day. Now
an abstraction of space –
all that food
bound in a fist of yarn
when the night began.

I hope you made it home, Anonymous.
Your stomach's contents –
a cairn to last night's exploits –
seem too personal
for my morning commute.
I try not to look, but do.

Man Whore

He wakes
        with a different woman's hand
                clapped
between his thighs
        like the curled paw of a hare
inveigled
           by the trap's false teeth.

He feels its weight,
        imagines the ripple
each hand might create   if skipped
           into a pool of water
                like a stone,

      the way the nails peck
like bird beaks
          at his skin,   the pauses between
                        the pecking,
the slick of lacquer   that squeals a colour
       he strains to remember
          from the night before.

I search for men like him,
        leave my mark
      like the singed thumbprint
                of a saint.

Vile Jelly

It would have been easy
to go sexy for Halloween
like that woman on *Come Dine With Me*,
who, when hungry, said things like,
'I am so ravished'
(when she meant 'famished').

sexy: that slinky adjective
followed by an unassuming noun
to describe things that aren't actually appealing at all –
a schoolteacher with a questionable past,
furloughed jail bait, an off-the-clock crossing guard –
but become so on Halloween.

You did not want me to be any of these things.
You said,
'what about your dignity, your originality?'
your tipped glass condescending
towards the table
in a reliquary of candlelight.

So, on Halloween night
I am Gloucester's eyeball, and you
are Cornwall's sword.

I am wrapped in a sheet, crouching behind
a circular cardboard cut-out,
you are yourself, in jeans and a t-shirt,
holding a boy's toy sword.

Eyeballs speak in movements –
a glance to the side, a twitch, a dilation,

but I am a fake eyeball
so I do not speak at all,

though every time you yell
'Out, vile jelly! Where is thy lustre now?'
and pierce me with your sword,
I hope you know my eyes are rolling.

Petit Socco

Kebab shop, bric-a-brac stalls: she loops
between lapis-hued clothing lines, through
courtyards with fountains, trespasses riads
hunting out carved initials – any sign she lived there
during the comatose years when Westerners
crossed the Strait to smoke and fuck.

The rooms of has-been smoke dens now fucked
by a different type of tourism: ceiling fans loop
overhead so that wealthy westerners
feel comfortable as they voyeur through
the time warp looking glass. No hash here
(unless you want it)! Free love emaciates in the riad's

refurb. Gone is the stained glass, the myriad
of *zellige* tiles, hookah pipes, the master fucking
his harem of wives. I hang on the tail feathers
of her fringe-trimmed coat as she loop-de-loops
through one Moorish door and out through
another, telling me: 'We aren't those kind of Westerners.'

Even as she says it, I know I'm the hollowest
shade of her bohemian ideal. She inspects the riad's
floorboards for strawberry blonde strands sloughed
from the ghost of her gorgeous mane – 'the one fuckable
thing about her.' She recalls dinners of *loup
de mer*, mint tea, clementine wedges to fill their

hunger as we skip from this roof to that, tether
ourselves to a faith that is anything but Western.
How many milky-eyed moons have looped
the earth since her return to the riad
where the Dutchman asked her to fuck
to the call to prayer? She was gobsmacked through

and through. Not surprised, I tell her I hope she threw
him out, wondering what really happened to father
our journey to this rag torn and fucked
little city. Like a patient daughter feigning awestruck,
I embrace the muddle of ochre-tinted riads,
clasp the hand of Fatima on the silk-cord looped

around my neck. At nightfall, we move west
past the withered stork nests on the walls of riads.
The clap clap clap of men fucking on loop.

Exhibit A, Exhibit B

A: Medieval Text Display

A black velvet backdrop
within a cube of darkness.

Even with the spotlight,
words lose their meaning
in calligraphy so old.

The ancient text floats
the way stars appear to;
the way the drowned rabbit did
in the Jacuzzi that night,
brushing against our bodies.

B: Float Lab

Because I am now a starfish,
I think of Sandra's body
splayed out in the brownstone
two buildings down from here –
a needle stuck in her arm
the way a golf flag
marks the hole.

I used to love the pale skin
of heroin addicts, not those
who used for years,
but the newer ones,
their eyes so wide and unblinking
they could swallow the world.

I wonder what all the people
we used to know are doing.
I picture them stumbling off the beach
after the drum circle
in the middle of summer,
all of us floating together
in a tank of Nag Champa
and sweat –
the scent of Dogtown contained –
the way it was a million lives ago.

I think of you in the tank next to mine –
      weightless,
though less so in thought;
of what we didn't say
in the car on the way here
when the hard words
lodged in the throat
and nothing wrenched out.

After the Drought

The downpour sluices the bluffs;
mud pools along the trail.
Kids make games of skipping
over them. Janet is in my head
worried that the earth cannot absorb
the overindulging rain.

Wherever she is, she'll worry all day
mistaking sink taps
                            for waterfalls.

If You Love Him, Let Him Sleep

Ambien worshippers pay to sleep like the dead:
I lift my phone every half hour to trawl nail polish products,
plan the Ayurvedic cleanse, read 'What Your Sleeping Position Says
About Your Love Life' and 'Pictures That Prove Cats Are Secret Agents.'

This false light stirs you, sends the dog to the leather couch.
My boredom prescribes small challenges: I bristle your ear hairs with my pinkie
trying to avoid the surrounding snail of skin, check to see how closely
my hand can confront your breath before you twitch.

There is nothing you can say between the closing and opening of shutters
that I don't already know by listening to your exhalations –
sometimes I mirror the tiny motor of your lips, the tilt of your head,
your chin doubling up, and wait for recognition.

Miscarriage

I'm told
the moonstone
I carried
in the palm
of my hand
could not alone
will a living thing
to term,

and the eggs
consumed
upside down
on a Sunday
once held
the same possibility
for which I grieve.

Sometimes things
that do not exist
are real –
the way my ears
hear Etta James
sing "Cadillac"
not "At Last",
or how the opening
acoustics
to "Little Wing"
are, to me, a mimesis
of drowning.

Announce this: today,
the colour of failure
is the robin's
sanguine throat.

More Asleep Than Dead

Before long
you will spend more time
in the garden with the barbecue
burning the drying brush –
a christening of grey-blue ash –
until you're ankle deep in it.

And I will be inside
retreating further into rooms
you don't enter anymore,
and for some time we will pretend
like two people orbiting
the same sinuous truth –
that ribbon of diaphanous silk –
like the Romans at Pompeii who,
overcome by shock,
still believed the crops
were just burning.

Elegy of the Sandcastle

If hearing is the last faculty to go,
I need to believe your last moments weren't besieged

by the lady down the hall with the plastic doll pleading, 'please don't take my baby!'
or the Catholic nurse muttering 'Miss Evelyn, go to the light you wretch'

because you mocked her foreign accent with your Southern drawl
that stretched vowels into long afternoons on your daddy's porch in the Ozarks

where you learned as a girl how to make insults skip
from your lips with the air of a compliment – something I could never do.

In your last moments, I need to believe you heard the gulls overhead
and the sound of the ocean rocking the shore with a swell;

our voices buoyant as we held you in our hands
weaving you with the sand between our fingers,

the wet mixture dripping into turrets and caverns of mud and kelp;
the kitchen colander that blockaded the castle until completion.

I need to know the last sound you heard was the crash of surf
splashing over our toes, our ankles and shins –

that final burst of winter that carried you away,
retreating from us like the sound of rolling pebbles.

Fractals of Depression

There is nothing written in blue
        that cannot be forgotten
like the blue of the nursery
        whitened by sun wash.

We turn towards and away,
        towards and away
from the past, words cling to our lips,
        the flap of wood shingles —

blue moon, living room,
cat in the cradle
        and the silver spoon.

(We liken this to a game of Mad Libs
        where the crucial moments
are always parenthetical).

When we speak,
        we speak in circles
fencing the blue
        of the palest emotion

that is also a sagging grey sky.

Scar

She waters the cyclamen –
her hand like a stork's beak
delivers packages of ice
from her vodka tonic.

At the vanity, she plucks
long static teardrops
from her ears,
places them in the jewellery box
the way a child,
or the memory of one,
is put to bed.

Backstage

when my bread belly
wastes
from the habit
of denial
and the dark whip
inside of me
is somehow fed
in the process

when I tourniquet
my words
so that 'unravelled'
ravels again, 'inchoate'
slims to a whole

when I'm so thin
you can no longer
see me
unless the light
fractures
the windows
just so

watch me be as lithe
as airborne dust
that settles
on the necks
of androgynous swans
suspended
from the rafters

Metamorphosis

These caterpillar days,
this drudgery, the slow turn
of a season.

The moon squatting in my belly
dictates the tide
of unseen things; the woman
I have known for years
pads around on swollen feet –
the width of her tightrope widening.

When the kilo sack of oven chips
is empty, my birch tongue
lashes a hundred insults at you
then curls up in tears.

What is it we do
after swapping sides of the bed?
I watch you inhabit
my sleep. Light through
the window makes it harder
to know your face
with my hands; close your eyes,
conjuror, when you look at me.

My Father Tells Me to Get Married

Face paint made
from cephalopod ink,
carob nibs swapped in
for chocolate
buried in a dollop
of dough, velcro
laces for teens:
you taught us
the outer reaches
of convention.

Whole days went by
without walls defining
our space, except
the dogwood's boughs
draped in a corridor
around our car
with the windows
rolled down.

Scraped elbows
and bruised lips
healed by the science
of crystals: Rose Quartz
to soothe; Galena
for inflammation.

Ears to the dirt,
we listened
for a magnetic shift,
the reverse
of the earth clockwise,

knowing we'd never
hear it coming —

like now,
when from nowhere,
you assert my unborn child —
a soul migrant
of our distant relative —
cares about wedlock.
You're stroking my finger,
and I stare at you
with a mouthful
of flies.

Mauna Loa

Fissures warp the surface,
sulphur surrounds the roots
of silversword and palm.
We hear the pop
of foliage stunned by lava.
We make lists as we walk
of the things I am not supposed to do
(like this), register
the temperature of the earth
against each footstep, wind our way
to where the molten flow
meets the ocean. I will tell him
he witnessed it inside of me
tangentially, remembering
how my mother said the same.
Pele's Hair streams downwind
in the distance, a reminder
to walk the way we came.